The Seven Women Every Woman Should Know

Valencia Belle, BS, RN, BSN, MSFS

Copyright© 2016

All Rights Reserved

Unauthorized reproduction of the contents of this manuscript are prohibited by law, and may not be done without the express written consent of the author.

*There are seven women **EVERY** woman should know.*

These women impact your life by commission or omission.

They are either adding to or subtracting from your life in ways that you must pay attention to and be aware of at all times.

Not acknowledging their presence or existence can prove harmful and maybe even deadly.

Harnessing their power can occasion greatness.

Table Of Contents

Chapter 1:
Woman #1: The Woman Above You 1

Chapter 2:
Woman #2: The Woman Below You 5

Chapter 3:
Woman #3: The Woman In Front Of You 9

Chapter 4:
Woman #4: The Woman Behind You 13

Chapter 5:
Woman #5: The Woman To The Left Of You 17

Chapter 6:
Woman #6: The Woman To The Right Of You 21

Chapter 7:
Woman #7: The Woman Within You................25

Valencia Belle's Biography 29

Woman #1: The Woman Above You

She is your best self, your higher purpose and power.

She does what's right.

She has character and integrity.

She builds others up instead of tearing others down.

She does not gossip or get involved in pettiness.

She hates drama and avoids mess.

She meditates.

She prays.

Word To The Wise: The more time you spend with this woman, the less time you'll find yourself involved in discussions with people who waste both valuable time and energy, commodities that you cannot replace if you lose them, because they cannot be bought or sold.

Take Away Point: Always CHOOSE to be YOUR BEST SELF – TRUE to who you REALLY are!

Woman #2: The Woman Below You

She is the woman that you may not personally know or appreciate.

She has made sacrifices untold for you to exist and persist.

She is the reason that you are seated in the position you currently hold today; whether you know it or not, appreciate her or not, or even acknowledge her contributions to your life.

She has cried, and literally almost died, while painstakingly trailblazing the path of greatness that you're travelling on with ease right now.

She has bent her shoulders and chosen to let you walk up her broken back so that you, now, can stand tall.

She has believed in you, even before you were born, and realized that she had to excel so you wouldn't fail.

Woman #2: The Woman Below You

Word To The Wise: Find her! Hear her stories of trial and triumph. Learn from her. Thank her. You owe it to her to be great. Greatness is what she expects from you simply because that is who she was for you. She was your ninja-warrior-goddess-fairy-godmother, even though you didn't recognize her or appreciate her sacrifice.

Take Away Point: You OWE it to her to be GREATER than she has ever been, because you have opportunities now that she will never have, and possibilities that she could never have dreamed of.

Woman #3: The Woman In Front Of You

She is your mentor.

She is your guide.

She is the woman who knows where you are headed.

She also knows how to take you there.

She has already accomplished in the past what you're trying to accomplish in the present.

She's BEEN THERE, BELIEVED THAT and DONE THAT... a LONG TIME BEFORE you even thought about doing it.

She will PUSH you towards GREATNESS. She will definitely get on your LAST NERVE in her attempts to bring out the best in you.

She seems INVINCIBLE in emotion, IMPENETRABLE in strength and UNREASONABLE in her demands.

She makes you FORGET everything that you think is IMPORTANT for your life and re-arranges your entire life's AGENDA.

Until ...

You see her CHEER for you when you achieve your goal...and CRY for you when you receive second place when everyone knows you should have won first.

She knows exactly what you are capable of, and is RELENTLESS in her PURSUIT of your FUTURE GREATNESS.

Word To The Wise: LISTEN to her! Stop being PRIDEFUL. She can teach you how to be HUMBLE – when you are the best in the Nation…and the worst in the State. She can teach you how to win GRACEFULLY, how to handle fame TACTFULLY, and how to be a WOMAN on a MISSION with MERCY.

Take Away Point: Because she has been "abase and abound", she can show you how to truly have mercy, with yourself and with others, on your way to the top. How you handle and deal with people better than you, as well as those not as talented as you, determines how long you remain a part of ANY team. Use your mentor's WISDOM. Learn from her MISTAKES. Do not buy a life lesson that she's already paid for with EXPERIENCE.

Woman #4: The Woman Behind You

She is the little girl who wants to be you... ALL THE TIME!

She IDOLIZES the ground you WALK on.

She cannot see any of your FLAWS.

She thinks you are MAGIC...and PERFECT!

She patterns EVERYTHING she does after you.

She studies you for all the RIGHT reasons.

When she grows up, if you have done your job in mentoring her right, she will be your MINI ME.

Word To The Wise: Do not disappoint her. Live a life that she can look up to and EMULATE. Make the most of your time with her. Take time to be around her. Show her where you came from. Never forget her. Remember that she was once you. Hopefully, when you were growing up, the woman you idolized was there for you – actually carved time out of her hectic schedule to be there just for you. Do not ever believe that you have the luxury of not being a role model; that the decisions that you make now do not affect those watching you. Every cause has an effect. Sometimes, those who admire you the most never work up the courage to confront your GREATNESS for many years until after they have established their own identities. It can be VERY INTIMIDATING to meet your idol face to face. Do not leave the little girl who adores you STARSTRUCK; take her by the hand and let her touch and feel your GREATNESS.

Take Away Point: Let the little girl behind you be like the moon. Let her stand in the brightness of your greatness as the sun and reflect your light until she learns how to shine on her own. Do not be intimidated by her shine as it increases in brightness and intensity. She has been studying your greatness for a while. Be advised that, in the end, the same little girl who studied you might outshine you if you stagnate your own personal growth and fail to challenge yourself to continuously learn new things.

Woman #5: The Woman To The Left Of You

This woman studies you too...but for all the WRONG reasons.

Simply put, she wants to BE you.

If she could, she would REPLACE you.

She CANNOT, however, because she has not paid the COST to be the BOSS.

She will lie, steal and cheat.

She will do just about ANYTHING to insure that she wins.

She will stop at NOTHING to hurt you as she claws her way to the top.

She wants to DESTROY your very existence and erase your REMEMBERANCE.

She is jealous and hateful.

She is downright mean and evil.

She will befriend you, gain your trust and remain in your presence to learn everything about you. And then, when you least expect it, attempt to use your weaknesses and secrets against you.

Woman #5: The Woman To The Left Of You

Word To The Wise: FORGIVE HER! Know that there is a thin line between love and hate. If you do not focus on the Woman Above You, you could very well turn into her if you are not careful. Jealousy and envy are reserved for those who assume that the world owes them something. Stop living in FALSE ENTITLEMENT! Life does not owe you ANYTHING, but can give you EVERYTHING! If you are not willing to WORK HARD for what you want, do not expect to gain a free ride from other people's efforts. Everyone has the capacity to CHANGE – for the better or for the worse. Change requires CHOICE. Sometimes, the best personal choice for dealing with a person like her is to CUT HER OFF and LET HER GO. Learn to wear people like loose clothing. Your favorite sweater in the 3rd Grade does not always fit you in the 10th Grade. THINGS CHANGE. PEOPLE CHANGE. LIFE GOES ON.

Take Away Point: Never try to defend yourself against her lies. The truth will always surface. Give her time and space. If you are not sure about her, watch and pray. Given sufficient room, she will either grow and add to your life, or simply go. You do not have to convince a real friend to like you, or to stay in your life. If you choose to forgive her, FORGIVE HER. The only way that your friendship and association with her will continue is by your choice to completely forget the past. If you cannot forget her past mistakes and the offenses she has done to you completely, simply MOVE ON. When a person repeatedly shows you who they really are, BELIEVE THEM!

Woman #6: The Woman To The Right Of You

She is your "Ride or Die Chick".

She's your "Sister from Another Mother".

She knows ALL your secrets…and never SNITCHES.

She would "take a bullet for you" – as they say - or at least not let you go into a fight alone.

Truth be told, she would not allow you to be entangled in the drama of a fight AT ALL.

She would NEVER let you get caught up, or caught off guard.

She would help you AVOID anything that might hurt you now, or your reputation in the future.

She is quick to dismiss or cut off anyone who has anything but positive things to say about you.

She is COVENANT – Her bond is not easily broken.

She has seen you at your WORST...and did not care.

She tells you the TRUTH ABOUT YOURSELF. While everyone else is LYING, saying that you are ALL THAT to your face while making fun of you behind your back, she will ALWAYS BE TRANSPARENT and TRUTHFUL in her assessment of you.

If you needed it, you could have WHATEVER she HAD – NO QUESTIONS ASKED.

You can CRY AROUND HER, TRUST HER WITH YOUR S.O.(significant other) and YOUR WALLET.

Woman #6: The Woman To The Right Of You

Word To The Wise: Covenant relationships are made in the bad times, not in the good times. If she is "down" with you when you fail, and everything is totally horrible, she deserves to be "up" with you when everything succeeds, and you're completely on top. She can handle your success and shine because she has success and shine of her own. She uplifts you when you are down. She knows how to calm you and help you recalibrate when you go from "0 to 100" REAL QUICK because of anger and frustration. You are blessed in life if you have one true friend like her. Cherish her.

Take Away Point: Do not try to force this friendship. Pray and ask God to send her to you. If you are a member of a team, know that you should treat every member of your team like she is the Woman to the Right of you. If you have team members who are like the Woman to the Left of you, know that unconditional love and unwavering acceptance can change the hardest of hearts in a group of solo individuals into a solid group of caring individuals willing to sacrifice themselves for the greater good of the team.

Woman #7: The Woman Within You

Who are you anyway?

What is your "Elevator Speech?" — The statement that introduces you to strangers and summarizes everything about you in 2 minutes or less.

What are your goals?

What are your dreams — your dream life, your dream career, and your dream college to attend?

What aspirations have you set to accomplish your dreams?

Do you have a Vision Board to daily gaze upon your positive future?

Word To The Wise: As a woman thinks, so is she. Whatever you think about yourself is true — positive or negative. It's called a self-fulfilling prophesy — you can have what you say — so watch what you say to and about yourself.

Take Away Point: Be your own best fan. Encourage yourself! Build yourself up. You are only given one life. This is not a "dress rehearsal" – this is the movie called "YOU" in REAL TIME. Be the star of your own Motion Picture Event! No one, absolutely no one, can do YOU like YOU can! Have skillful intention and downstream focus! Be FEARLESS in the pursuit of your dreams!

Valencia Belle's Biography

2016 Woman of the Year

Valencia Belle is a Scientist and Entrepreneur who has spent her career helping to shape young minds by opening up the possibilities of "STEM" careers in Science, Technology, Engineering and Math.

A native of Mobile, Alabama and a true scholar-athlete at heart, she began running track and field at the age of 5. At the age of 12, as an entering high school freshman, she began her first fee-for-service tutorial business assisting fellow students with ACT Prep in Science and Math. While attending Murphy High School, Valencia thrived in sports, civic service and in Science and Engineering. She was chosen as the Alabama SECME and one of 7 NACME

Scholars in the country, as the Bryant Jordan Region VI Scholar –Athlete Award Winner, as an Azalea Trail Maid (Yellow), as Varsity Track Team Captain and as the Homecoming Queen - all while competing as a Team USA TAC Junior Olympian at the age of 16.

Valencia received her first Bachelor of Science Degree from the University of Alabama, where she majored in Biology. There, she was a member of Freshman Forum, the Student Government Association and the Elliot Society. She served as the Variety Director for University Programs and as a charter member and Secretary of the XXXI Women's Honorary. She would make the Dean's and the President's Lists. She was also 2nd Runner-up and Miss Congeniality in the Miss Alabama USA Pageant. Valencia not only was chosen as a Distinguished University

Graduate, receiving the Bloom Award, one of the top three University honors given for improving inter-faith and inter-group relations, but was also honored as one of the University's first minority IRBP Summer Fellows at the National Institute of Allergy and Infectious Diseases' Laboratory of Infectious Diseases for the National Institutes of Health in Bethesda, Maryland.

Although less than 1% of all NIH researchers are women and/or persons of color, Valencia was awarded an IRTA Fellowship with the National Institutes of Health upon graduation from the University of Alabama. Her research focus was on the "Simian Immunodeficiency Virus," or SIV, in a special breed of monkey and how this virus was connected to HIV in humans. Her research team led by Dr. Vanessa Hirsch helped advance the development of genetic mapping for antiviral medications and vaccinations now made available world-wide to help those suffering with HIV. To increase access to high quality, cost effective healthcare and foster better interdisciplinary communication for positive patient outcomes, she developed a holistic, fully integrated, family system based healthcare model called "NAMES". This would lead to Valencia receiving coveted Research Awards from both the National Cancer Institute and the Pediatric AIDS Foundation for the community health and educational outreach initiatives she began in minority and rural communities in the greater Washington DC metro area, Maryland and Virginia.

Valencia would go on to complete a second Bachelor of Science Degree in Nursing from Virginia Commonwealth

University, and a Master's Degree in Family Studies and Systems Integration from the University of Maryland. Her research would eventually focus on the achievement motivation of African- American girls seeking "STEM" healthcare careers. At the VCU School of Nursing, she was awarded the Johnson and Johnson Breakthrough to Nursing National Award, the Mary Marshall Virginia Department of Health Award and was named the School of Nursing's "Black History in the Making" Award Recipient. At Maryland, she earned induction into Phi Delta Kappa International Education Honor Society. Her work would take her abroad, to the Dutch West Indies, to research the different barriers and lack of educational opportunities for minority girls internationally who dreamed of attaining "STEM" healthcare careers within the US.

Her work in the Dutch West Indies led to her being chosen to work at Duke University Hospital and assist with efforts for the Duke Global Health Initiatives through the Duke School of Nursing, where she was chosen as a State Finalist for the Albert Schweitzer Award.

Today, Valencia is once again based in Mobile as a Scientist and Entrepreneur. She is the principal research consultant and owner of the Obsidian Consulting Group, which focuses on enhancing educational opportunities for minority girls wanting careers in Healthcare, Science or Engineering. In 2009, Valencia spearheaded the Edith Mitchell Health Initiative (EMHI) in honor of her late grandmother who founded the first nursing program for African Americans in Mobile Alabama at Carver State Technical College, which is now the School of Nursing at

Bishop State Community College. Since its inception, the EMHI has awarded over 30 scholarships to deserving minority and female students seeking "STEM" healthcare careers at Bishop State and Tuskegee University. Volunteers from the EMHI's Nursing Academy of Achievers have given over 1,000 hours of free Nursing coursework and NCLEX tutoring for students enrolled in Nursing programs, have offered over 2,000 hours of complimentary ACT, Math and Science tutoring to aspiring high school students and have manned over 20 healthcare screenings servicing more than 4,800 clients through capacity building and community partnerships.

In 2015, after 26 years, Valencia reunited with her first professional African American female STEM mentor, Dr. Latitia McCane, Academic Dean of Bishop State, to launch a powerful educational pipeline that has occasioned the following four initiatives in just one year: 1) the launching of the S.C.H.O.O.L.S Program (Success Can Happen Out Of Low Scores) Academic Enrichment and Supplemental Education Services Company, which offers ACT Prep, STEM tutoring and "wrap-around" educational coaching services to advance graduation rates and college entrance, 2) the creation of the JEM Scholars Program (Jumpstart to English and Math), which offers Dual Enrollment to eradicate the need of remedial collegiate courses pre-admission while making college affordable through the completion of college credit during high school, 3) the GOOGLE [X] Diabetes / Life Sciences Division Research Study, where Valencia, as a member of the research team, offers minority participants state of the art biotechnology in the control and management of diabetes, and most recently, 4) the opening of the LSHSC (Leflore Student Health Services Clinic), which offers high quality, cost effective healthcare free of charge to students in a clinic run and manned by STEM healthcare degree seeking minority students from disadvantaged backgrounds. Please visit www.emhi.org for more information regarding these pioneering programs.

Valencia thanks her friends and family for allowing her to use her gifts to creatively blend social science, healthcare and education to change her world her way by bettering her community. To her grandmother, Edith Mitchell, the nurse-educator and community advocate, who instilled the pattern of selfless service; her father, Donald Belle, the professional athlete and community activist, who showed her the value of an athlete's heart filled with determination; her mother, Antoinette Belle, the biomedical lab analyst who first demonstrated that Black girls could and should pursue STEM careers; her little "big" sister, Anitra-Belle Henderson, the "general" of capacity building who encouraged her to dream big and be "fabulous" while making history; her eldest niece, Kierstyn Johnson, the global Gen Y "sparkle" who motivates her to do even more; and to the Women who have been life-long friends, colleagues, mentors and "village" mothers. Valencia's prayer is that she continues to make history in humble service to God and to her community.

For Speaking Engagements/Book Inquiries Please Contact:

schoolsprograms@gmail.com

Made in the USA
Columbia, SC
14 July 2024

38361634R00029